GUITAR *signature licks*

GUITAR INSTRUME[NTALS]

BY WOLF MARSHALL

ISBN 0-7935-9458-8

HAL•LEONARD®
CORPORATION

7777 W. BLUEMOUND RD. P.O. BOX 13819 MILWAUKEE, WI 53213

Visit Hal Leonard Online at
www.halleonard.com

GUITAR NOTATION LEGEND

Guitar Music can be notated three different ways: on a *musical staff*, in *tablature*, and in *rhythm slashes*.

RHYTHM SLASHES are written above the staff. Strum chords in the rhythm indicated. Use the chord diagrams found at the top of the first page of the transcription for the appropriate chord voicings. Round noteheads indicate single notes.

THE MUSICAL STAFF shows pitches and rhythms and is divided by bar lines into measures. Pitches are named after the first seven letters of the alphabet.

TABLATURE graphically represents the guitar fingerboard. Each horizontal line represents a string, and each number represents a fret.

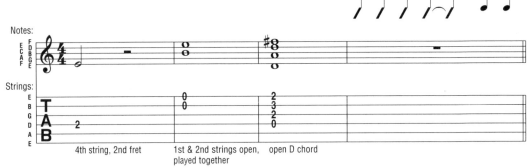

4th string, 2nd fret   1st & 2nd strings open, played together   open D chord

HALF-STEP BEND: Strike the note and bend up 1/2 step.

BEND AND RELEASE: Strike the note and bend up as indicated, then release back to the original note. Only the first note is struck.

HAMMER-ON: Strike the first (lower) note with one finger, then sound the higher note (on the same string) with another finger by fretting it without picking.

TRILL: Very rapidly alternate between the notes indicated by continuously hammering on and pulling off.

PICK SCRAPE: The edge of the pick is rubbed down (or up) the string, producing a scratchy sound.

TREMOLO PICKING: The note is picked as rapidly and continuously as possible.

WHOLE-STEP BEND: Strike the note and bend up one step.

PRE-BEND: Bend the note as indicated, then strike it.

PULL-OFF: Place both fingers on the notes to be sounded. Strike the first note and without picking, pull the finger off to sound the second (lower) note.

TAPPING: Hammer ("tap") the fret indicated with the pick-hand index or middle finger and pull off to the note fretted by the fret hand.

MUFFLED STRINGS: A percussive sound is produced by laying the fret hand across the string(s) without depressing, and striking them with the pick hand.

VIBRATO BAR DIVE AND RETURN: The pitch of the note or chord is dropped a specified number of steps (in rhythm) then returned to the original pitch.

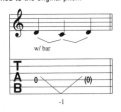

GRACE NOTE BEND: Strike the note and bend up as indicated. The first note does not take up any time.

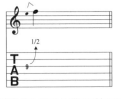

VIBRATO: The string is vibrated by rapidly bending and releasing the note with the fretting hand.

LEGATO SLIDE: Strike the first note and then slide the same fret-hand finger up or down to the second note. The second note is not struck.

NATURAL HARMONIC: Strike the note while the fret-hand lightly touches the string directly over the fret indicated.

PALM MUTING: The note is partially muted by the pick hand lightly touching the string(s) just before the bridge.

VIBRATO BAR SCOOP: Depress the bar just before striking the note, then quickly release the bar.

SLIGHT (MICROTONE) BEND: Strike the note and bend up 1/4 step.

WIDE VIBRATO: The pitch is varied to a greater degree by vibrating with the fretting hand.

SHIFT SLIDE: Same as legato slide, except the second note is struck.

PINCH HARMONIC: The note is fretted normally and a harmonic is produced by adding the edge of the thumb or the tip of the index finger of the pick hand to the normal pick attack.

RAKE: Drag the pick across the strings indicated with a single motion.

VIBRATO BAR DIP: Strike the note and then immediately drop a specified number of steps, then release back to the original pitch.

2

GUITAR INSTRUMENTAL HITS

CONTENTS

INTRODUCTION

Whether swinging, shredding, or simmering, instrumental rock guitar music is a staple of modern guitar lore. Born in the fifties as separate regional phenomena by bands that just wanted to rock without a singer, the art form evolved into a subgenre and finally a respected musical alternative, as well as a legitimate showcase for some of the form's most talented instrumentalists. This special *Guitar Instrumental Hits Signature Licks* edition chronicles the rise of the idiom and presents a compilation of its most beloved classics. Featured here is a blend of vintage guitar hits by the Ventures, Duane Eddy, and Link Wray; blues favorites from B.B. King, Freddy King, Stevie Ray Vaughan, and Albert Collins; rock offerings by Cream and the Allman Brothers; and more. So plug in, turn on, and join me for a trip through the ages, where we'll let the guitar do the talking.

—Wolf Marshall

DISCOGRAPHY

The titles in this volume came from the following records:

ROCK INSTRUMENTAL CLASSICS, Vol. 1: The '50s. (Rhino Records)
"Raunchy," "Rumble," "Rebel 'Rouser," "Guitar Boogie Shuffle," Sleep Walk"

COLLECTION, Larry Carlton. (GRP Records)
"Sleepwalk"

WALK—DON'T RUN—The Best of The Ventures. (EMI)
"Walk—Don't Run"

HIDE AWAY: The Best of Freddy King. (Rhino)
"Hide Away"

BLUES BREAKERS: John Mayall with Eric Clapton. (London)
"Hideaway"

SURFIN' HITS, Various artists. (Rhino)
"Pipeline"

THE BEST OF B.B. KING, Volume One. (Flair)
"(Ain't That) Just Like a Woman"

CROSSROADS, Eric Clapton. (Polydor)
"Steppin' Out"

DANCE OF THE RAINBOW SERPENT, Santana. (Columbia/Legacy)
"Song of the Wind"

A DECADE OF HITS 1969–1979, The Allman Brothers Band. (Polydor)
"Jessica"

TEXAS FLOOD, Stevie Ray Vaughan and Double Trouble. (Epic)
"Lenny"

COLLINS MIX: The Best of Albert Collins. (Pointblank/Charisma)
"Frosty"

THE RECORDING

Wolf Marshall: guitars
Mike Sandberg: drums and percussion
Michael Della Gala: bass
John Nau: keyboards
Bill Bixler: saxophones
Gary Ferguson: drums on "Lenny" and "Hideaway"

Drums recorded at Pacifica Studio and Ice Bone Studio
Overdubs recorded at Marshall Arts Music Studio
Digitally edited by A&M Music & Design

Produced by Wolf Marshall

Special thanks to Brian Vance and Max Ruckman at Gibson USA, Del Breckenfeld and Keith Brawley at Fender Musical Instruments, Jimmy, Julie, and Lisa at Dunlop Manufacturing.

RAUNCHY
(As Recorded by Bill Justis)
Words and Music by William Justis and Sidney Manker

Figure 1 – Theme and Guitar Solo

The golden age of instrumental rock began in the late 1950s. Spartan guitar-based combos replaced the larger swing bands of the previous decade, and rode the crest of the rock 'n' roll wave along with popular singers like Elvis Presley, Carl Perkins, Chuck Berry, and Ricky Nelson. Case in point is "Raunchy," a funky little rockabilly number, penned by Bill Justis and his partner, guitarist Sid Manker, in 1957, which is widely regarded as rock 'n' roll's first instrumental song. Justis was Sun Records' musical director back then, and rock 'n' roll mythology has it that Justis was forced to play sax on the date at the last minute when the session player didn't show. His rusty chops were responsible for the primitive sax sound heard on the track, which added much to its earthy charm. The tune reached #2 on November 18, 1957 and spent 14 weeks on the Top 40 charts. Photos from the period picture Sid Manker playing a late-1950s natural-finish Gibson ES-175 arch-top electric with P-90 pickups. This is most likely what we hear on the track.

"Raunchy" is appropriately titled. Visceral and grungy, it is essentially a 16-measure blues in D. Blues elements permeate the tune, most explicitly in the strict use of I, IV, and V chords of the genre and some characteristic harmonic gestures like the chord progression of measures 9–16. The head is built on a thematic bass-register guitar riff in D. This riff is played in the first position, makes use of open strings and a walking bass line melody, and is punctuated with a simple D chord—alluding to the country-blues style which influenced most of the Sun Records artists. It is decorated with a repeated bend on the fourth string which generates a minor-third/major-third pitch ambiguity in every occurrence of the figure—another obvious concession to the blues genre. Aspects of this seminal riff have been applied to countless hard rock and blues riffs ever since.

Manker's guitar solo is essentially rhythmic, and is based entirely on double stops and triads. He employs an aggressive, strummed articulation throughout, similar to Chuck Berry and the electric blues guitarists of the 1950s. The slurs in his solo are also idiomatic to this approach. Most of the double stops are fourth dyads or partials of the underlying D triad, and are fingered as barred shapes on the top three strings.

Shortly after completing his guitar work on "Raunchy," Sid Manker's career was over. News of his mother's death left him in a state of mental breakdown and he turned to heroin, which absorbed his life and the royalties from "Raunchy." He passed on from a heart attack in 1974.

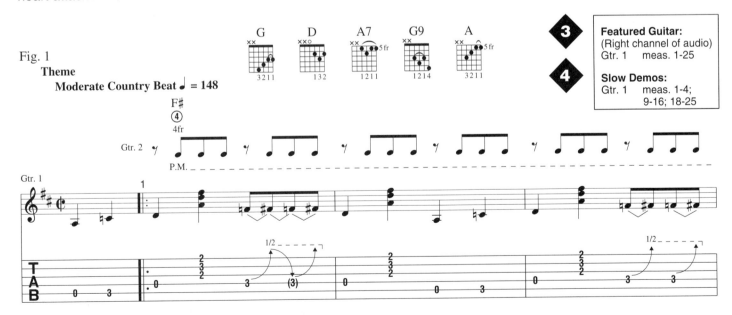

Featured Guitar:
(Right channel of audio)
Gtr. 1   meas. 1-25

Slow Demos:
Gtr. 1   meas. 1-4;
            9-16; 18-25

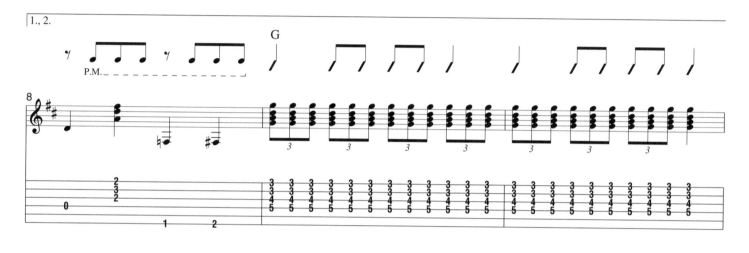

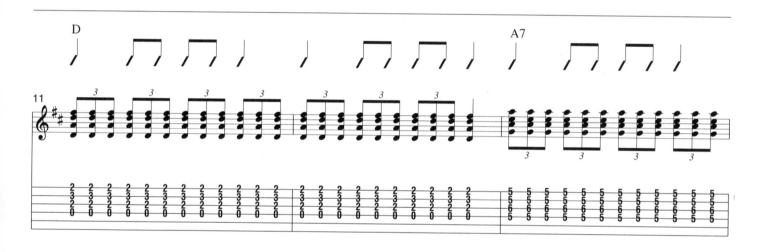

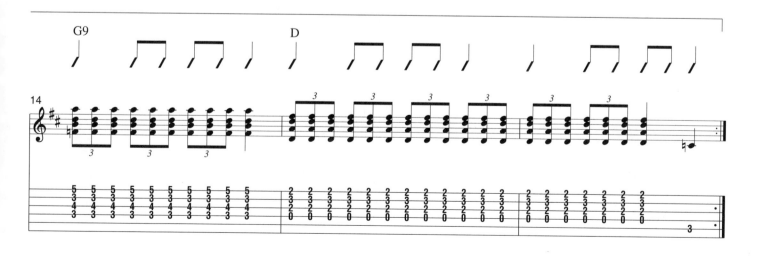

RUMBLE
(As performed by Link Wray and His Ray Men)
Words and Music by Link Wray and Milt Grant

Figure 2 – Theme and Guitar Solo

Link Wray is the missing link between the rock 'n' roll guitarists of the 1950s and the incipient hard rockers of the early 1960s. Wray's effect on seminal British rockers like Peter Townshend and Jeff Beck, both of whom cite him as an important influence, is profound. "Rumble" is his most memorable hit. One of rock's happy accidents, it was written spontaneously while Wray was playing a record hop in Fredericksburg, Virginia, and was asked to play a stroll. He didn't know any and instead made up "Rumble" on the spot. The tune reached #16 on May 12, 1958 and remained on the charts for 10 weeks. Recently, "Rumble" enjoyed a well-deserved revival when it was featured in the 1996 sci-fi epic *Independence Day.*

Based rhythmically on a plodding, slow-dance groove called "the Stroll," "Rumble" is nothing less than the precursor of modern hard rock. Sinister and sparse, the bulk of the tune is made of simple open chords (D, E, A, and B7), and works somewhat like a lop-sided 11-measure blues in E. The theme is based on a series of slow-moving open chords. Two D chords in quarter-note rhythm precede the sustained E and A chords in measures 1–7. The last phrase, in measures 9–11, is comprised of an arpeggiated B7 chord and the most rudimentary minor pentatonic lick in rock history. The latter, in measures 10 and 11, is played in the first position and is a pure E minor pentatonic scale descent in triplets. Bonehead simple but highly effective, it proves one of rock's most central tenets: It's not what you do but how you do it.

On the recording, Wray played his 1953 Gibson Les Paul and a Premier amp with a large 15" speaker and two small 6" tweeters. He reputedly achieved the prototypical fuzz-distortion sound by punching holes in his speaker with a pencil. Don't try this at home! He further enhanced the sound with generous amounts of reverb and amp tremolo.

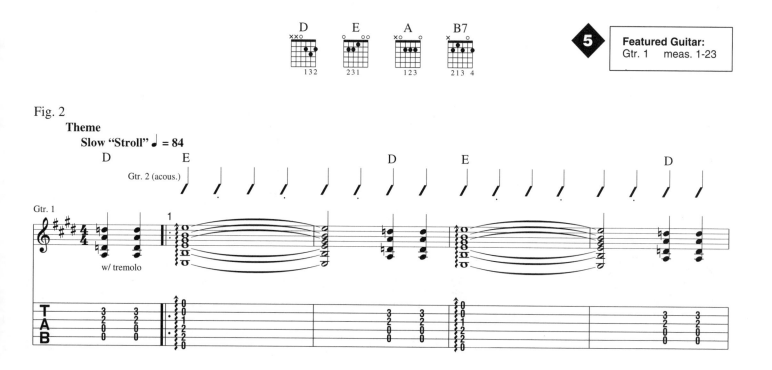

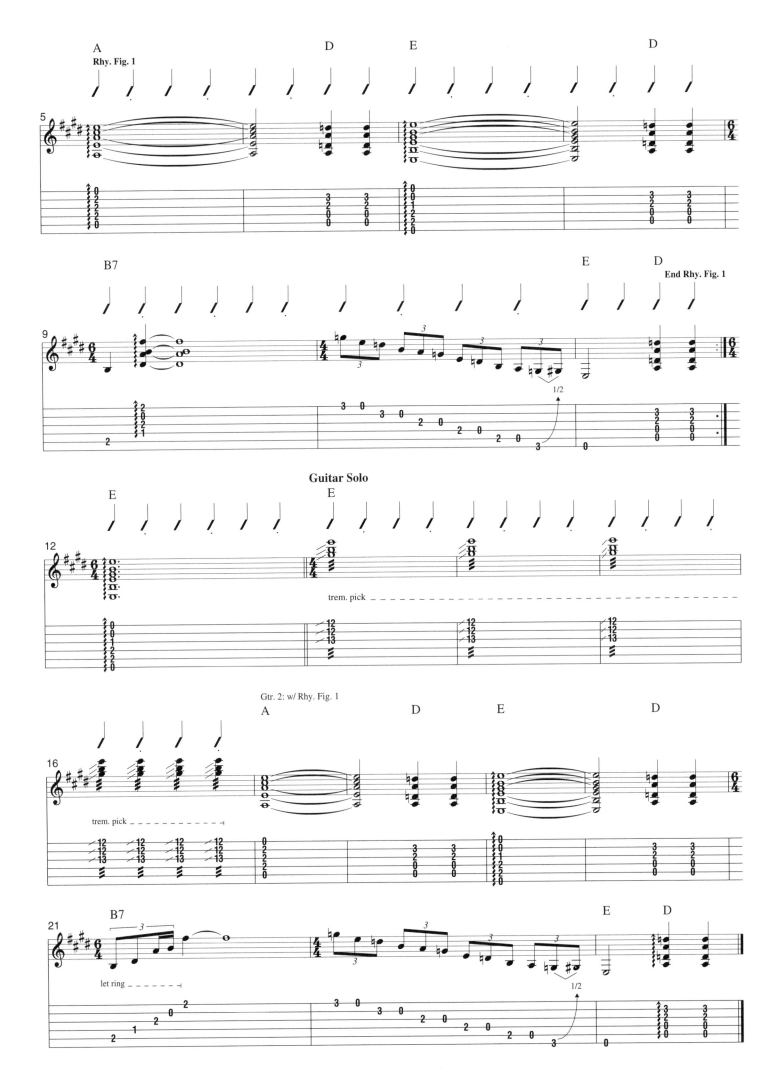

REBEL 'ROUSER
(As Performed by Duane Eddy)

By Duane Eddy and Lee Hazlewood

Figure 3 – Theme

The 1950s and 1960s were an era dominated by rock and pop singles and front men. Unique in his specialty, Duane Eddy stood out as the first rock 'n' roll instrumentalist to successfully market consecutive hit singles and to front a band. "Rebel 'Rouser" was his first hit and set the tone for many future releases. With this track, Eddy developed a highly effective formula, nicknamed "twangy guitar," which crossed over easily into the pop market. This would become his signature sound: a simple, accessible melody played in the bass register of the guitar, often decorated with string bends and liberally colored with reverb, echo (via an empty 500-gallon water tank), and other effects. At producer Lee Hazlewood's insistence, Eddy did not improvise solos on his hits, which heightened the pop ethic at work in his music. "Rebel 'Rouser" reached #6 on July 7, 1958 and resided in the Top 40 for 12 weeks.

"Rebel 'Rouser" is structured like a simple pop song of the era. Built around a 16-measure folk-style theme, it is rhythmically very straightforward—comprised almost exclusively of quarter notes and whole notes tied to halves. The harmonic framework is also very straightforward, confined exclusively to I, IV, and V chords. The theme melody is minimal, utilizing simple diatonic lines and primary triad arpeggios. Each 16-measure theme is repeated verbatim throughout the tune in different keys. Even this changing tonal movement is kept very simple. The successive choruses of the theme are modulated one half step higher with each new repetition—from E to F to G♭, and finally to G.

On "Rebel 'Rouser," and his other early hits, Eddy played a Gretsch 6120 Chet Atkins guitar with DeArmond pickups and a Bigsby vibrato tailpiece. He plugged into a modified Magnatone amp which was boosted to 100 watts and equipped with a 15" JBL speaker and a tweeter. On the track Eddy used an old DeArmond Tremolo Control, a small stand-alone motor-driven device, to produce the trademark tremolo effect.

6 | **Featured Guitar:** Gtr. 1   meas. 1-34

Fig. 3

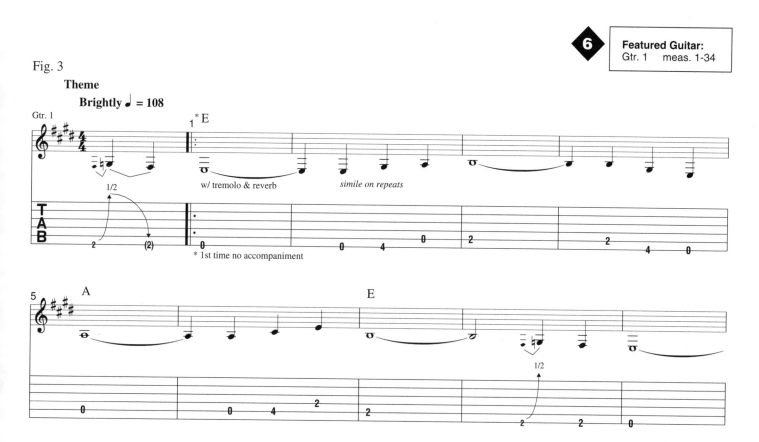

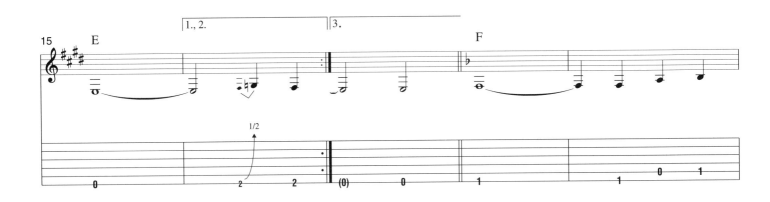

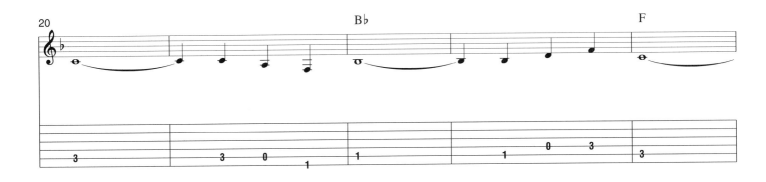

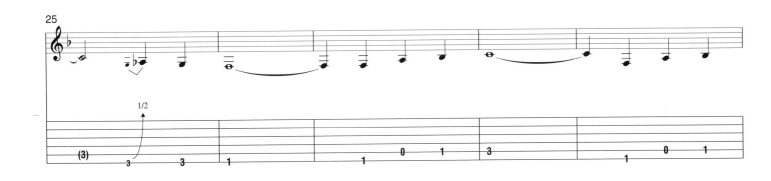

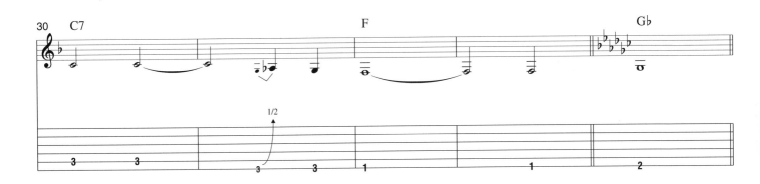

GUITAR BOOGIE SHUFFLE
(As Performed by The Virtues featuring Jimmy Bruno Sr.)

By Arthur Smith

Figure 4 – Intro, Head, and First Guitar Solo

Rewriting history can be a daunting and problematic business. Such is the case with "Guitar Boogie Shuffle." History incorrectly credits Frank Virtue as the guitarist on the track and further ascribes the tune to Arthur Smith. Its inclusion in this collection provides us with an ideal opportunity to set the record straight. Here is the real story as recounted and substantiated by his son, Jimmy Bruno Jr. (who incidentally is one of the most compelling jazz guitarists on the scene today—check him out). In the 1940s and 1950s, guitarist Jimmy Bruno Sr. played with a bassist named Frank Virtue. Virtue was not an accomplished musician but had an uncanny knack for obtaining work. As times were tough, Bruno stayed with this band. In the 1950s, Virtue built a small recording studio in his house and there they recorded "Guitar Boogie Shuffle" as the Virtues. The members on the date were Jimmy Bruno Sr. (guitar), Tom Friday (drums), Ralph Federico (piano) and Frank Virtue (bass). Contrary to popular belief, Bruno Sr. was the composer of the music but failed to copyright his work, thinking that the boogie-woogie riff was public domain and not realizing that his arrangement granted him ownership rights. A self-made millionaire, Arthur Smith, who had recorded a different version on acoustic earlier, wound up with the rights and the credit. Virtue's lawyers and the record company saw to it that Bruno received 10% of 1% for his efforts. Bruno discovered this while on tour and quit on the spot, vowing never to record again and further stating that Virtue would never have another hit song. "Guitar Boogie Shuffle" reached #5 on March 23, 1959 and remained in the Top 40 for twelve weeks. It was the Virtues' one and only hit.

"Guitar Boogie Shuffle" is a 12-bar blues in E (which sounds a half step lower in E♭) founded on a swing-inspired triplet feel. In the intro, Bruno plays a ground-finding pattern in eighth-note rhythm on the open low E string to get things rolling. His sound during the head is treated with generous amounts of slap-back echo. The head [A] is based on a four-note ascending-descending melody (E–G♯–B–C♯: root–third–fifth–sixth) which is the quintessential boogie riff of the period—in essence, a left-hand boogie-woogie piano pattern transferred to the bass register of the electric guitar. Variations of this figure are moved through the I–IV–V changes of a simple 12-measure, three-chord blues progression. Note the use of G (the seventh) over the A chord in measure 7, and the use of D (the sharp ninth) over the B7 chord in measure 10.

The interlude [B] is based on a catchy ostinato riff made of a quarter note and an eighth-note triplet. The triplet contains the ascending chromatic motion B–C–C♯, which strengthens the sixth (the goal of this motion) in the figure. This riff, like the main theme, is taken through the 12-measure blues form with slight variations.

Bruno's improvised solo choruses in [C] and [D] reveal the close relationship of late 1940s swing jazz and early rock 'n' roll. You could describe these phrases as "Charlie Christian licks in a jitterbug context." His lines are certainly jazz-oriented, based primarily on the E Major scale (E–F♯–G♯–A–B–C♯–D♯), with characteristic passing-tone chromaticism in measures 26, 28, 41–43, and 45–47, and arpeggios in measure 32–34. Specific references to Charlie Christian's style are heard in the explicit use of the sixth tone (C♯) in measures 27–29 and measure 45, the inverted mordent embellishing figure in measure 31 (a Lester Young motive popularized by Christian on the guitar), the staccato rhythmic motive in measures 34–35, and the dominant-ninth lick in measures 42–43. Unlike Christian's style, Bruno's licks are devoid of string bends and contain no overt references to Texas and Oklahoma blues guitar styles.

On the recording, Jimmy Bruno Sr. played a honey blonde Gretsch hollow body (probably a 6120) with DeArmond pickups, and plugged into an Ampeg Gemini II amp.

[Before playing along with Figs. 4 and 5, tune down 1/2 step with track 7]

Fig. 4

Tune Down 1/2 Step:
① = Eb   ④ = Db
② = Bb   ⑤ = Ab
③ = Gb   ⑥ = Eb

8 Featured Guitar:
Gtr. 1   meas. 1-49

9 Slow Demos:
Gtr. 1   meas. 1; 2-13;
14-25; 26-49

Intro   **A** Head

14

C Guitar Solo (First Chorus)

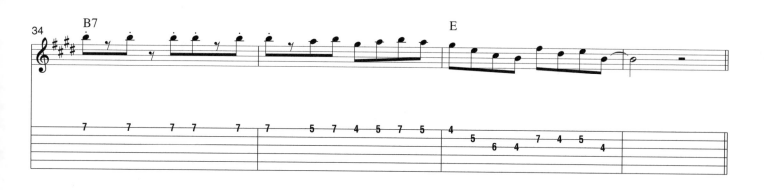

D (Second Chorus)

Figure 5 – Second Guitar Solo

Bruno's second two-chorus solo in [E] and [F] continues and elaborates in the swing and jazz vein. He re-enters with a langorous slurred melody which slides from low to high on the fretboard in measures 1–4. The riff-based melodies in measures 7–8 give way to a swinging string of eighth notes in measures 9–12. The use of the E♯ lower neighbor note to emphasize F♯ in measure 10 is a familiar jazz device. The rolling ostinato riff in measures 13–15 is the only blues mannerism in the solo and creates a strong climax in the tune. Bruno plays the three-note motive (G–A♭–B) in triplets as a slurred figure to produce a great sense of forward momentum over the E chord. This phrase influenced many a guitarist in rock, blues, and jazz, including an upcoming Philadelphia bop player named Pat Martino who used similar ostinato figures in his solos. His closing lines reprise many of the jazz-based ideas found in his first solo, including Christian-influenced licks like the E6 arpeggio in measures 19 and 22, chromatic passing tone passages, and inverted mordent figures.

10 **Featured Guitar:**
Gtr. 1   meas. 1-24

11 **Slow Demo:**
Gtr. 1   meas. 1-24

Fig. 5

Guitar Solo (First Chorus)

SLEEPWALK
(As Performed by Santo and Johnny)
By Santo Farina, John Farina and Ann Farina

Figure 6

Instrumental pop hits reached a zenith in 1959. Twenty-eight various instrumentals charted that year, many of them guitar-driven rock 'n' roll numbers. One of the loveliest and most haunting rock instrumentals of all time was released in 1959 when Santo and Johnny laid "Sleepwalk" on the pop world. Santo (steel guitar) and brother Johnny (electric guitar) Farina from Brooklyn, New York, co-wrote this dreamy instrumental ballad with their sister Ann, and it was their only hit, but it was a tremendous record with a remarkable atmosphere. Apparently the buying public thought so too—"Sleepwalk" attained the coveted #1 position on August 17, 1959, remained in the Top 40 for 13 weeks, and is a bonafide rock classic. With its vocalesque steel guitar melody, "Sleepwalk" comes closer to a vocal pop song than any other instrumental record of the era—which may be one reason several auspicious guitar players have gravitated toward it in recent years. In the 1980s it was a staple of Los Lobos' repertoire and also received notable covers by Larry Carlton and Jeff Beck.

"Sleepwalk" is structured like a 32-measure, AABA-form song: two 8-measure "verse" sections, an 8-measure bridge, and a final 8-measure "verse." It epitomizes the "slow-dance" rock rhythm feel of the 1950s. The accompaniment and central pulse is anchored by a triplet-based 12/8 meter, which is also the heartbeat of tunes like "Earth Angel," "Sixteen Candles," "The Great Pretender," "In the Still of the Nite," and many others. Another familiar aspect is its recurring harmonic pattern of I–vi–IV–V, the so-called "ice cream changes," which are played throughout by Johnny in barre chords as the main accompaniment figure in the A sections. An interesting and effective departure from stock "ice cream changes" is the use of an Gb minor (iv) chord throughout, which adds a melancholy touch.

The melody is composed of simple diatonic lines which draw on the Db major scale (Db–Eb–F–Gb–Ab–Bb–C) and the Gb melodic minor scale (Gb–Ab–Bbb–Cb–Db–Eb–F). Note the common tones Db, Eb, F, Gb, and Ab. The juxtaposition of the two scales creates one of the most memorable themes of the era.

This transcription and the accompanying performance on CD are an adaptation of the original version with the Santo steel guitar part arranged for standard guitar. The part is eminently playable on guitar, as Jeff Beck ably proved in his 1985 cover for the *Porky's Revenge* soundtrack (check it out on the *Beckology* box set). The thematic slide motive, in measures 2–3 of the intro and throughout the song, is arranged for standard-tuned slide guitar. The Hawaiian-style steel guitar slurs and vibrato have been converted into bends, dips and shakes with the vibrato bar, as in the Beck rendition.

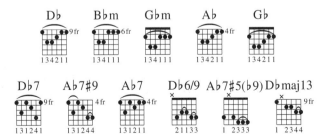

Fig. 6

Intro
Slow Rock Ballad ♩. = 63

SLEEPWALK
(As Performed by Larry Carlton)
By Santo Farina, John Farina and Ann Farina

Figure 7 – Guitar Solo

Fast forward to 1981. No guitar instrumental volume would be complete without an offering from stylist Larry Carlton. His touch, sound, and musicianship on the instrument are truly legendary and highly influential. Larry made his appearance in the L.A. studio scene of the mid-1970s on records by Steely Dan, Joni Mitchell, the Crusaders, Ray Charles, and countless other appreciative pop and rock clients. By 1978 he was an established solo artist and probably the most well-known "jazz-rock fusion" guitarist in the world. In 1981 Carlton covered "Sleepwalk" with high-production trappings on his *Sleepwalk* album and it has remained a favorite in his repertoire. The track featured studio cohorts Terry Trotter and Don Freeman on synthesizer and keyboards, Pops Popwell on bass, and John Ferraro on drums. A perfect vehicle for Carlton's distinctive style, distinguished by slinky string bends, jazz-oriented harmonic sophistication, and overt melodicism, "Sleepwalk" is exemplary—a modern instrumental masterpiece.

"Sleepwalk" documents Carlton's first recordings with a solid-body guitar. Previously, "Mr. 335" (as he was nicknamed in studio circles) had employed a Gibson ES-335 to produce his unmistakable instrumental voice. For this date, he played a custom-made Valley Arts Strat, which defined his crisp new sound of 1980s. In this period he made the transition from the trademark Mesa-Boogie amps of the seventies to his currently-preferred Dumble amps.

"Sleepwalk" showcases Larry's inimitable solo approach. Renowned for his colorful blend of jazz, rock, funk, and blues styles, Carlton mixes them all skillfully in a marvelous 14-measure improvised ride. For the solo, he modulates to E♭ from the original key of C and plays against a recurring vamp of E♭maj7–Cm7–Fm7–B♭7 (I–vi–ii–V), essentially the verse changes. Larry plays with great dynamics and infinite nuance using a finger plucking technique instead of a normal plectrum attack. Carlton's noteworthy single-note lines are closely linked to the individual chords of the progression. He sets up an intriguing juxtaposition of two distinct elements, tuneful major sounds and grittier blues-oriented minor sounds, as a general strategy in the solo. Melodious E♭ major pentatonic (E♭–F–G–B♭–C) licks are played almost exclusively over the E♭ (I chord), while the Cm7 (vi chord) frequently receives the G♭ note (flatted 3rd) for a nice bluesy effect, as in measures 5, 7, 11, and 13. Chromatic passing tones in measures 1, 4, 9, and 12 reveal Larry's jazz inclinations, as do the altered-dominant chord lines in measures 2 (B♭7♭9[♯5]) and 12 (B♭7♭9). By contrast, the abundant string bends and singing vibrato throughout, and the riff-based licks in measures 7–8, attest to his blues leanings.

13 Featured Guitar:
Gtr. 1   meas. 1-15

14 Slow Demos:
Gtr. 1   meas. 1-15

Fig. 7
Guitar Solo 2:08
Slow ♩. = 67

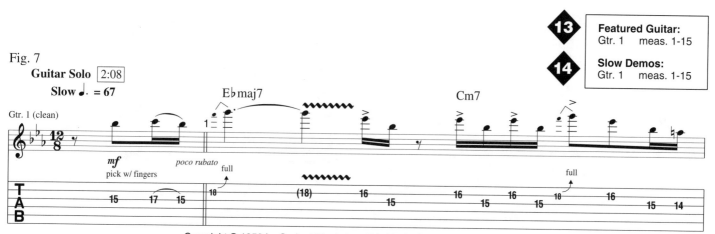

* Played ahead of the beat.   * * Played behind the beat.

WALK DON'T RUN
(As Performed by The Ventures)
Words and Music by Johnny Smith

Figure 8 – Theme and Bridge

1960 marked the beginning of a new decade and a new era in instrumental rock. The classic instrumental combo style emerged with the efforts of the Ventures, a quartet from Tacoma, Washington, who crystallized the work of their immediate predecessors and made an enormous splash with an unlikely hit: "Walk Don't Run." "Walk Don't Run" became a hit via a circuitous route. It was written by jazz guitarist Johnny Smith, learned from a Chet Atkins version on *Hi Fi in Focus*, and simplified to fit the rock combo format of two guitars, bass guitar, and drums. The Ventures played down the complicated bop-Baroque bent of Smith and Atkins, replacing its jazz-oriented conception with a straight rock beat and a rudimentary harmonic approach. Bob Bogle and Don Wilson played lead and rhythm guitars and Nokie Edwards played bass on the original track, though by the time of its remake in 1964, Bogle and Edwards had switched roles. Many listeners deem "Walk Don't Run" the quintessential instrumental guitar classic of all time—and how can you argue its importance? It was their biggest hit, #2 on July 25, 1960, and the model for countless imitators to follow—a record that changed history and the way a guitar sounded and was played.

The arrangement for "Walk Don't Run" is as simple as it gets, an attribute which is much of the Ventures' charm. Wilson played the basic rhythm part with parallel major barre chords for the A–G–F–E progression in the intro and head, and used open chords in the first position. The theme melody is based on the A natural minor scale (A–B–C–D–E–F–G). Bogle played the melody in the first position taking advantage of open strings and simple folk-style fingerings. Following the lead of his role models, Chet Atkins and Duane Eddy, he used the vibrato bar throughout to color the phrases, as in measures 6, 9, 14, 16–17, 21, and 23–24. This embellishment varies from a subtle vibrato to an actual half-step pitch bend.

The definitive early Ventures sound was achieved with Fenders. Bogle and Wilson played a Jazzmaster and Stratocaster respectively and plugged them into blond Bandmasters or tweed Vibrolux amps, often employing the built-in tremolo effect. Their heavy Fender presence enticed many peers and the entire subgenre of surf music to base their instrumental combo sound on Fender tones.

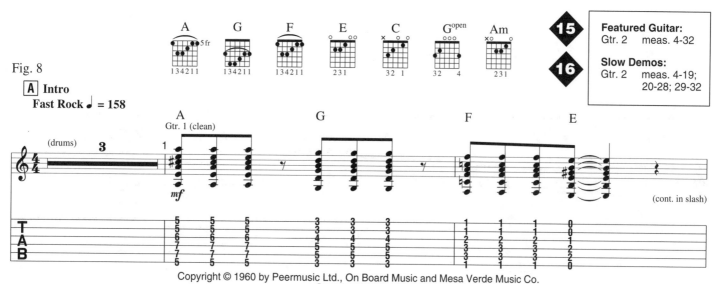

HIDE AWAY
(As Performed by Freddy King)
By Freddy King and Sonny Thompson

Figure 9 – Head, Guitar Solo, and Interludes

The blues guitar factor was a given in rock instrumental music since its inception (readily apparent in the harmonic progressions of tunes like "Raunchy," "Guitar Boogie Shuffle," and "Rumble" among others), but the true blues instrumental didn't really crack the Top 40 until the appearance of Freddy King in the early 1960s. King's blues instrumentals of the era became standards in the genre and, of the many tunes he made famous, "Hide Away" is unquestionably the most enduring guitar classic. It was a crossover hit for Freddy, reaching #5 on the R&B charts, and ultimately #29 on the Top 40 charts on April 3, 1961. Today, "Hide Away" remains hearty jam fare in clubs everywhere—a must-know tune in the annals of blues and rock. It is also one of the catchiest pieces ever in the repertoire—distinguished by memorable riffs, well-crafted feel changes, and King's highly accessible guitar style.

"Hide Away" is a 12-bar blues in E. Freddy treats each 12-measure chorus differently, thus each becomes an event in itself. He follows this arrangement outline: [A] head, [B] elaborated head or solo, [C] interlude ensemble riff in half-time feel, [D] second interlude (a tempo in shuffle feel) with a bass line riff, [E] stop-time breaks, [F] "Peter Gunn" riff in straight time.

The head [A] is a landmark Freddy King moment. Here he turns simple first-position E major pentatonic (E–F#–G#—B–C#–) and open-string blues licks into a piece of blues-rock history. King's turnaround phrases from "Hide Away" in measures 11–12 of [A], [B], and [D] have become required essentials in blues guitar coveted by countless players. The fifth chorus [E] contains stop-time breaks that showcase the famous "Hideaway" chord, E9, in its unique three-note voicing, as well as the familiar sliding 6ths lick in measures 3 and 4. By contrast, low-register bass-line-type riffs dominate choruses [C], [D], and [F].

Freddy King had a unique style and sound. He played with a thumb pick and a metal finger pick, instead of a flat pick or bare fingers. King favored Gibson thin-line guitars (ES-345s and 355s primarily) for the bulk of his career, after beginning on a gold-top Les Paul with P-90s in the 50s. He played various Fender combo amps and, like Albert Collins, expressed a preference in later years for the 100-watt 4x12 Quad Reverb.

17

Featured Guitar:
Gtr. 1 [A] - [F] meas. 1-12

Slow Demos:

18

Gtr. 1 [A] meas. 1-12;
　　　[C] meas. 1-12;
　　　[D] meas. 1-12;
　　　[E] meas. 1-8;
　　　[F] meas. 1-12;

Fig. 9

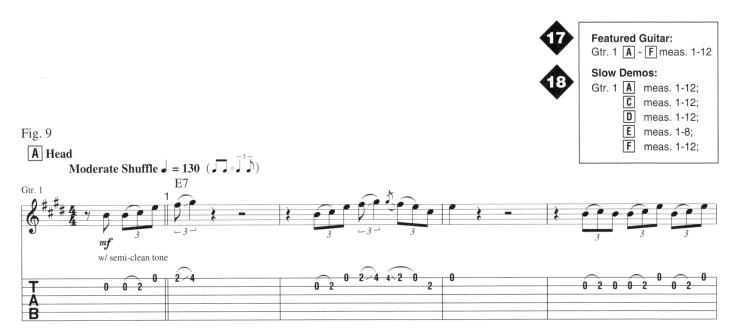

B Guitar Solo 0:22

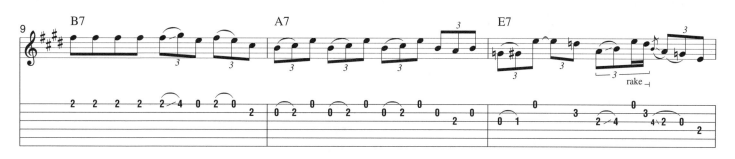

C Interlude 1 0:44

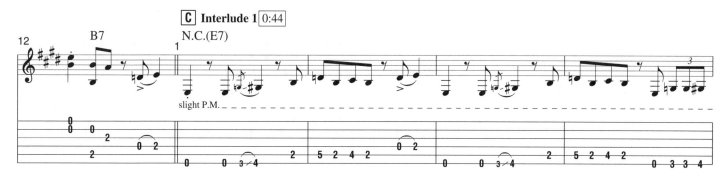

HIDE AWAY
(As Performed by The Bluesbreakers with Eric Clapton)

By Freddy King and Sonny Thompson

Figure 10 – Head, Interludes, and Guitar Solos

Fast forward to 1965. Eric Clapton made "Hide Away" a signature piece of the blues-rock genre when he included the instrumental in the watershed recording *Blues Breakers: John Mayall with Eric Clapton*, one of the most influential recordings in rock history. This was definitive British blues—the fusion of London's earliest hard rock experiments with imported Chicago blues styles—and remains the yardstick by which much of today's blues-rock music is measured.

In "Hide Away," Clapton supercharged the more laid-back Freddy King version, converting it into a vehicle for his fiery playing. He retained many of the most notable features of the instrumental—faithfully including a note-for-note rendering of the head melody (played, however, in the higher ninth position), the "Hide Away" chord (E9), and stop-time breaks in [E], measures 1–2, and its various feel changes. Clapton personalized the piece significantly in his solos. In fact, his innovative solos in [B], [D], and [E] laid the early foundation for many of today's rock lead licks. Note the use of both the E minor pentatonic (E–G–A–B–D) and E major pentatonic (E–F♯–G♯–B–C♯) scales—often in conjunction—at different points in the improvisations, and the unfettered movement all over the fretboard. Eric chose to further modify the cover by substituting a "Memphis" theme in [F] for the "Peter Gunn" riff of King's version.

Clapton made sonic history on this track, and the entire Mayall album. When he played his Les Paul Standard into an overdriven 50-watt Marshall "Bluesbreaker" 2x12 combo amp, it was a musical first in the genre. He set the stage for the guitar sound of modern electric blues, hard rock, and heavy metal in the coming years, influencing the tone of his contemporaries (Beck, Page, and Hendrix) as well as significant future players like Gary Moore and Eric Johnson.

19 Featured Guitar:
Gtr. 1 [A] - [F] meas. 1-12

20 Slow Demos:
Gtr. 1 [A] - [F] meas. 1-12

Fig. 10

[A] Head
Moderate Shuffle ♩ = 144

Gtr. 1

* Key signature denotes E Mixolydian
** Chords derived from organ part.

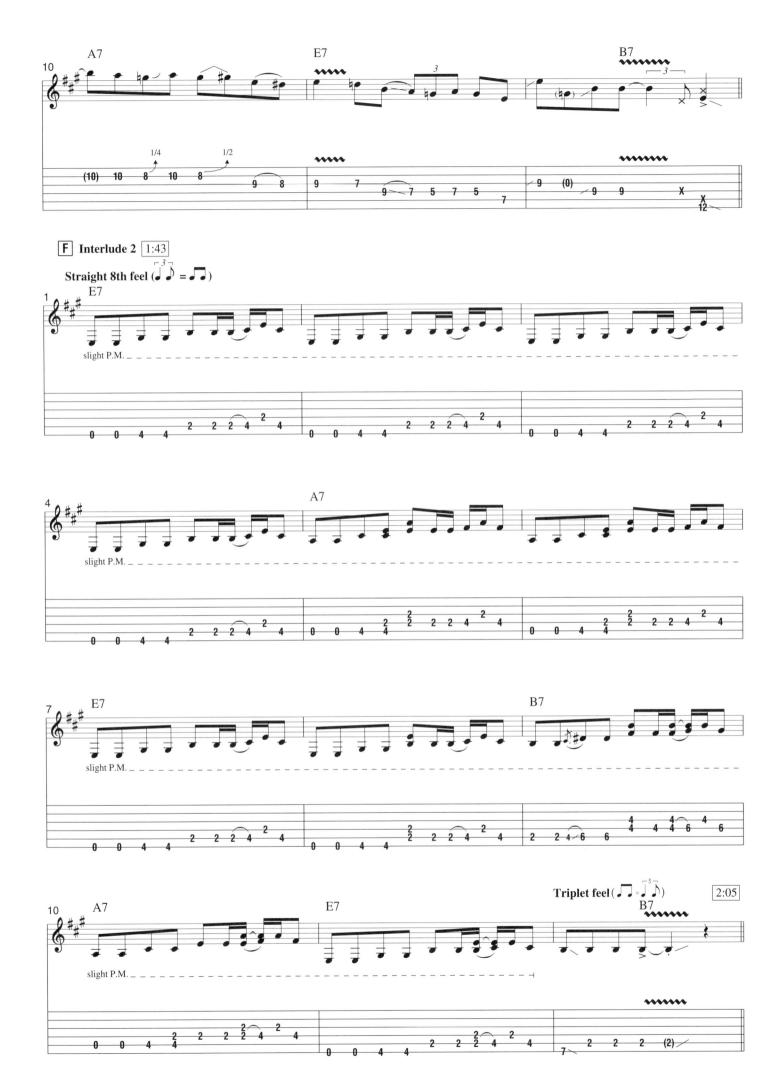

PIPELINE
(As Performed by The Chantays)
Words and Music by Bob Spickard and Brian Carman

Figure 11 – Head and Bridge

The instrumental sound and style we know as surf music has its roots in early rock 'n' roll, R&B, country, and pop. It grew out of the instrumental rock scene of the fifties and early sixties, fostered by the efforts of the Ventures, Link Wray, Duane Eddy, and others. By 1961, surf music was an established musical form in the southern California beach communities, and spread rapidly across the country to touch both the pop culture and the youth subculture everywhere. It affected the sound of rock and pop records, film scores, and even TV commercials, and continues to do so to the present day.

March 1963 was marked by the release of the Chantays' "Pipeline," an instrumental tribute to Hawaii's pipeline waves. The track reached #4 on the Top 40 charts and swam in the Top 40 for 11 weeks. It embodied many of the most obvious aspects of the surf guitar style—most notably tremolo-picking, a wet spring-reverb sound, and allusions to ethnic melody and modal harmony. The Chantays added a new wrinkle in the form of percussive palm muting for an extreme staccato effect throughout. To meet the demand for heavy muting, Fender issued both their top-of-the-line Jaguar guitar and the Bass VI in 1963 with built-in mutes at the bridge.

"Pipeline" is best remembered for its percolating, muted bass-register guitar riff, played by Gtr. 2. This is heard immediately after the trademark tremolo-picked and palm-muted glissando run in the intro. The riff uses the outline of an E minor chord (root–5th on the sixth and fifth strings) plus an alternating G note, and is repeated constantly throughout the tune in the head. The head or theme, played by Gtr. 1, is a 36-measure section which develops a simple diatonic melody against the i (Em) and iv (Am) chords in E minor. In the final six measures of the theme melody, Gtr. 1 plays a similarly sparse line over a B7–C–B7–C–B7–Am chord progression. Gtr. 2 plays a purring, single-note figure on the fifth string as an important backing part.

The 16-measure bridge is played over a Spanish flamenco-inspired chord progression of Am–G–F–G–Am–G–F–Em. Here, Gtr. 2 plays a tremolo-picked and palm-muted bass-note line—more a drum beat on guitar than a riff or chord figure—primarily in sixteenth-note rhythm, which enlarges on the pattern established in the head.

Though Brian Carman recalled using a low-budget Kay guitar on the original recording, the sound of surf music is glassy Strats, Jazzmasters, and Jaguars, early sixties Fender tube amps (especially the piggy-back Showman, Bandmaster, Bassman, and Tremolux models), and tons of reverb, as exemplified in "Pipeline."

Featured Guitars:
Gtr. 2   meas. 1-4
Gtr. 1   meas. 5-26
Gtr. 2   meas. 27-42

Slow Demos:
Gtr. 2   meas. 1-3
Gtr. 1   meas. 5-19
Gtr. 2   meas. 27-34

Fig. 11

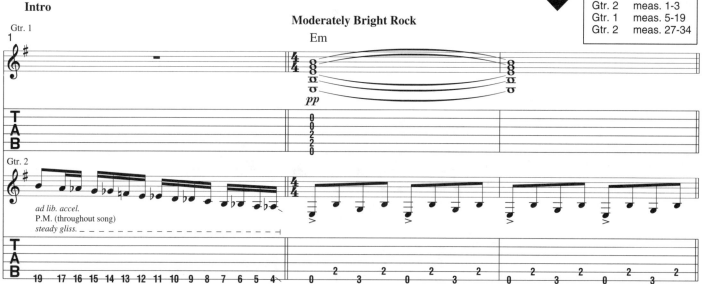

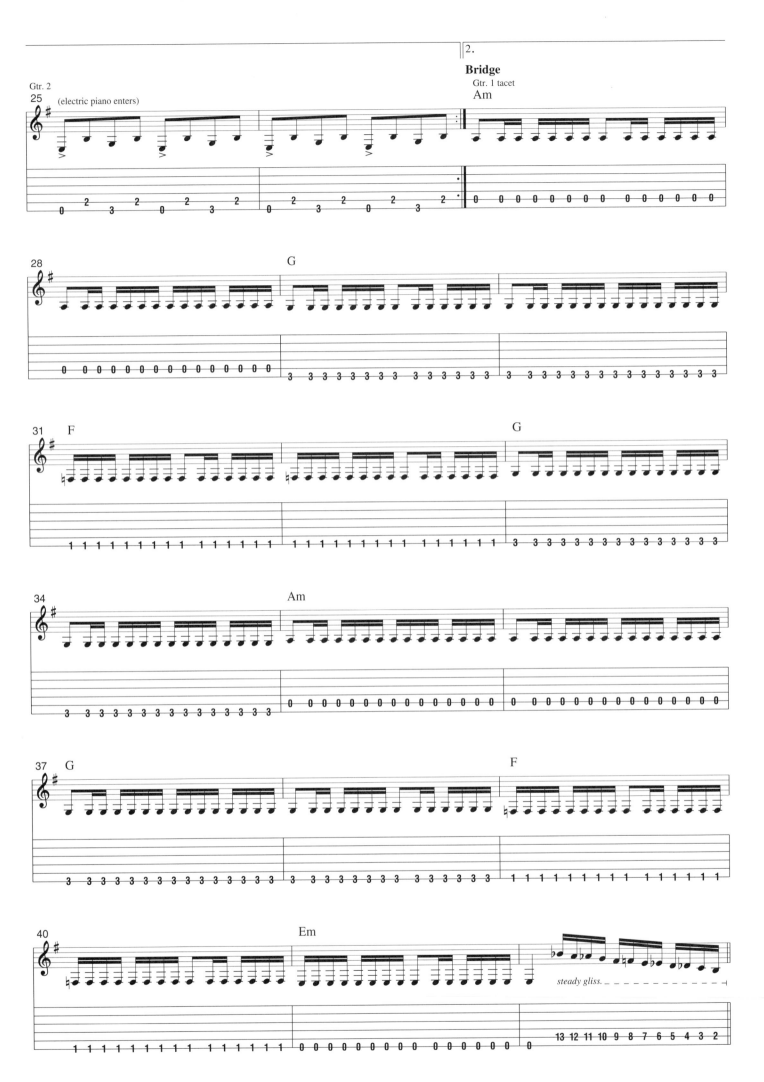

(AIN'T THAT) JUST LIKE A WOMAN

(As Performed by B.B. King)

Words and Music by B.B. King

Figure 12 – Intro, Head, and Guitar Solos

The number of major guitarists who cite B.B. King as an influence would fill several books. Suffice it to say that his music and guitar style affected musicians on both sides of the Atlantic, and exerted a substantial and influential role in shaping the blues-rock sounds of the future. His stamp can be detected on almost every electric guitar soloist after 1965, particularly the succeeding generation of players like Eric Clapton, Mike Bloomfield, Jimmy Page, Carlos Santana, Duane Allman, Larry Carlton, and Stevie Ray Vaughan. While the majority of his repertoire was vocal, the "King of the Blues" issued one of the most swinging blues instrumentals of the era in 1966 with "Ain't That Just Like a Woman." A true guitar masterpiece, it is probably his most extended "blowing" piece of the early years.

"Just Like a Woman" is a 12-bar blues in G. The piece is constructed like a vocal blues song with King's guitar, Lucille, replacing the voice and telling her story instrumentally. It is set in a fast shuffle feel and features a decidedly swing-based blues approach. The tune begins with a marvelous opening guitar break in the intro [A]. This four-measure unaccompanied solo presents King's scale-combining approach in capsule form. He combines notes from the G major pentatonic scale (G–A–B–D–E) and the G minor pentatonic scale (G–B♭–C–D–F). This is a mixture frequently found in his playing and lays the foundation for much of his soloing in "Just Like a Woman." It is also a strategy pursued regularly by devotees like Clapton, Santana, and Page.

The head [A] is a 12-measure section which establishes the song's shuffling groove. King lays back with sparse chord jabs on the "and" of beat 3 of each measure, a familiar syncopation in the swing-blues genre and one which works beautifully with this overall rhythmic pulse. The chords (primarily a G6 triad) are played with a well-accented staccato articulation which is typically found in his comping approach. A second guitar plays a boogie-woogie bass riff in the background.

The points of interest are numerous and noteworthy in his first three solo choruses, letters [C] through [E]—each a 12-bar blues progression in G. Briefly, King begins by introducing riff-like question-and-answer licks in the first four measures of [C] (measures 17–20). These emphasize the seventh (F) and are played in the middle register of the guitar. They are an important thematic element in the solos heard in varied form in [D] (measures 29–30) and in [E] (measures 41–44). A classic B.B. King motive is found in measures 28, 31, and 39. This signature lick is a sliding figure which involves a slur into a unison note (G) in a higher position (sixth position) from a lower position (the blues box in the third position). The slide typically receives King's famous hummingbird vibrato, as in measures 31 and 39. The use of the 6th (E) and ♭3rd (B♭) is significant in the licks of [D] (measures 33–36) and [E] (measures 45–48). Here King plays off the background shout vocal part, filling in the spaces around the figure. The E and B♭ are used interchangeably against both the C7 and G7 chords, as 3rd and 7th of C, or 6th and ♭3rd of G. The E and B♭ notes are also used for the bent tritone double stop in these phrases, a notable blues cliché worked into the solo. In measures 36–40 King adopts a contrasting swing-jazz conception with a more sophisticated longer line in eighth-note rhythm. Here he employs chromatic approach tones, interval jumps, and syncopation. Note that the E note in measure 37 strongly implies the ninth of D7, a jazz-based harmony. An elaboration of this melody is found in the next chorus ([E], measures 49–52).

By this time B.B. King had established his trademark guitar voice with a semi-hollow thinline Gibson guitar—usually the top-of-the-line ES-355, currently made as the "Lucille" model. He plugged into small Fender combo tube amps and used a slightly overdriven, semi-clean tone to add a vocalesque, singing quality to his lines.

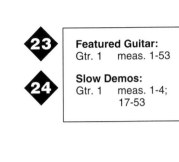

Fig. 12

STEPPIN' OUT
(As Performed by Cream)
Words and Music by James Bracken

Figure 13 – Head and Guitar Solos

"Steppin' Out" was an eagerly-awaited showcase number in Cream concerts, and served to engender the reputation of the power trio as virtuoso improvisers and Clapton as a guitar god. Written by Peter Chatman (alias blues pianist Memphis Slim), it is a true Eric Clapton signature tune and a bonafide instrumental rock classic. There are many superb versions in Clapton's catalog. This one comes from the middle of Cream's most active period and was recorded on January 9, 1968, for a live BBC radio show. It finally surfaced twenty years later on the *Crossroads* collection.

"Steppin' Out" had always been a chance for Clapton to stretch out and play at length, which he does convincingly in this track. Throughout, his playing is relentless, fluid, and exciting. He digs into the tune's up-tempo groove with a vengeance, coming up with a strong rendering of the main theme (head) followed by a fiery set of improvisations in the solo.

The first solo is played over four fast choruses of a 12-bar blues in G, and exemplifies Clapton's scale-combining approach. The first chorus (0:13) is mainly in G minor pentatonic (G–Bb–C–D–F). The F♯ neighbor-tone figure in measures 17–19 is a well-known Clapton melodic motive. The second chorus (0:26) mixes operative notes (Bb and C) from G minor pentatonic into an exemplary G major pentatonic (G–A–B–D–E) lick in measures 25–27. The third chorus (0:38) alternates between pure minor and major pentatonic sounds: G minor in measures 37–38, G major in measures 39–40, G minor in measures 41–43, and G major in measures 44–47. The fourth chorus (0:51) features angry, bent double stops in measures 49–50 before returning to a G major pentatonic line in measures 50–51. The remainder of the section is in G minor pentatonic, and closes with a decisive slide into the downbeat of the bass solo. Also noteworthy in the solo is Eric's strong rhythmic delivery which conveys an astonishing confidence and adds authority to his blistering lines.

25 Featured Guitar:
Gtr. 1   meas. 1-60

26 Slow Demos:
Gtr. 1   meas. 1-12;
13-24; 25-36;
37-48; 49-60

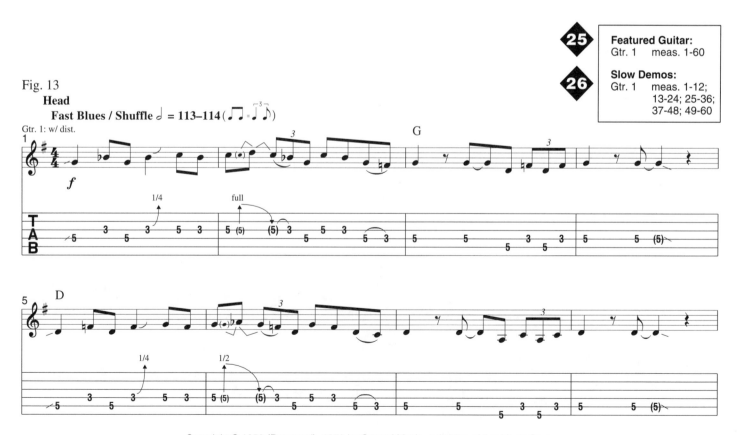

Fig. 13
Head
Fast Blues / Shuffle ♩ = 113–114

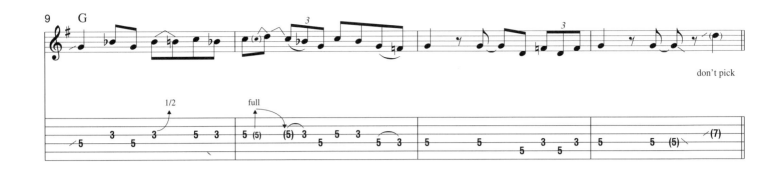

Guitar Solo (First Chorus) `0:13`

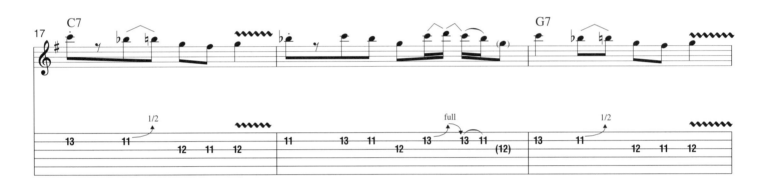

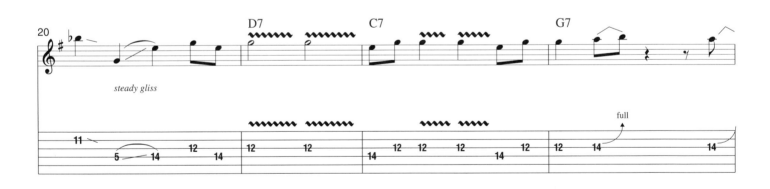

(Second Chorus) `0:26`

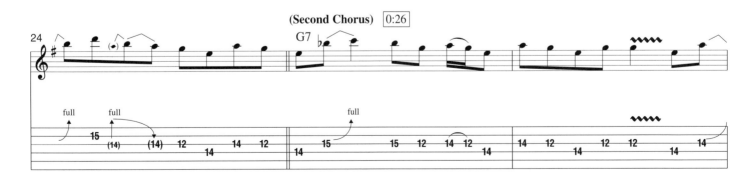

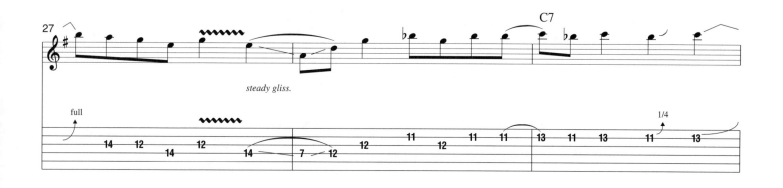

(Third Chorus) `0:38`

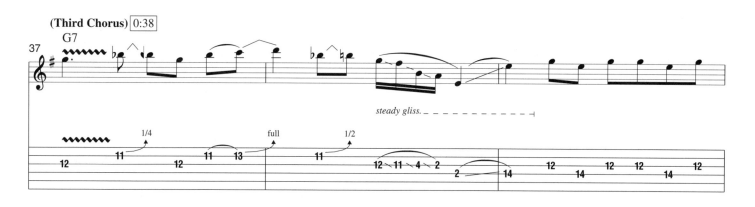

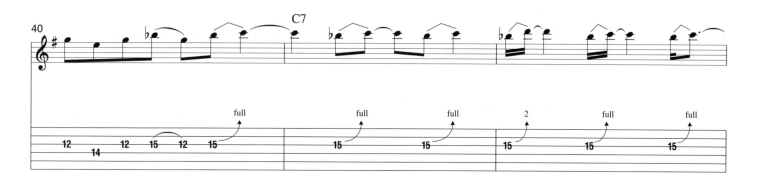

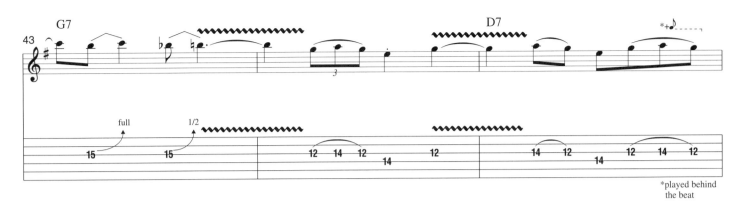

*played behind
the beat

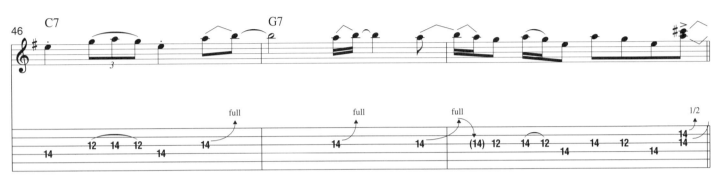

(Fourth Chorus) 0:51

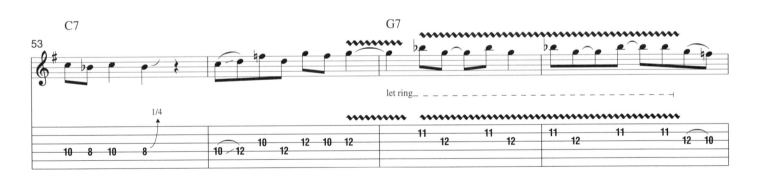

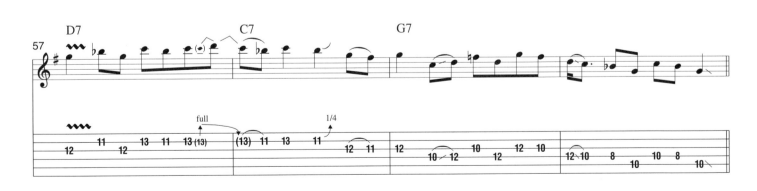

SONG OF THE WIND
(As Performed by Santana)
Words and Music by Gregg Rolie, Neal Schon, and Carlos Santana

Figure 14 – Intro and Guitar Solos

Carlos Santana is blessed with one of the great instrumental voices of the guitar. Truly unique, innovative, and immediately recognizable, he speaks through the guitar and can sing a melody on the strings like no one else. Additionally, his early experiments with jazz and ethnic elements expanded the vocabulary of blues-rock music in the late 1960s and 1970s, precipitated the fusion movement, and anticipated the arrival of world music by over a decade. "Song of the Wind" is a classic Santana instrumental of the era. This landmark track is from *Caravanserai* (1972), his last record with the classic Santana band and represents an important phase of his lifelong musical journey.

In contrast to most of the tightly structured instrumentals in the rock, blues, and pop genres (and in this volume), "Song of the Wind" is essentially a long, free-form jam. There is no clear form, no distinct head or theme melody, no structural contrast sections like bridges or interludes, and no definite length to solo choruses. Instead, it is based entirely on a simple two-chord vamp of Cmaj7 to Fmaj7. Over this repeated nuclear pattern, Santana and guitarist Neal Schon create a beautiful piece of guitar improvisation—trading solo licks and phrases and passing musical ideas back and forth. The intro represents an awakening in which the guitar enters tentatively as if from a deep sleep, after eight suspended measures of atmosphere and texture. By measure 19, the guitar begins a series of improvised solos played with more animation. Here they introduce punchy blues-based lines and riffs in sixteenth-note rhythm, and let loose a pure stream of improvisational consciousness. From this point on, licks become melodies, melodies become stories, and stories are woven into the fabric of this large and unified musical tapestry.

The solo lines are generally modal, and are based on both the C major pentatonic scale (C–D–E–G–A) and the C major scale (C–D–E–F–G–A–B). The only non-harmonic tone (F#) is found in measures 9, 10, and 39. Though the lines can be analyzed as scales, the playing transcends any strict adherence to scalar playing. Instead, melodies contain moods not modes, alternating between blues licks with pitch bends and vibrato, straight diatonic lines, and primarily rhythmic phrases.

On *Caravanserai* Santana achieved his signature sound with a sunburst Gibson Les Paul guitar and two stock Fender Twin amps. Schon played a matching Les Paul and Fender amps.

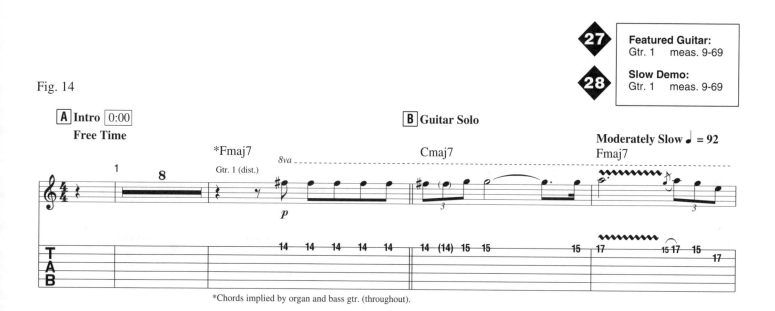

27 Featured Guitar:
Gtr. 1   meas. 9-69

28 Slow Demo:
Gtr. 1   meas. 9-69

Fig. 14

*Chords implied by organ and bass gtr. (throughout).

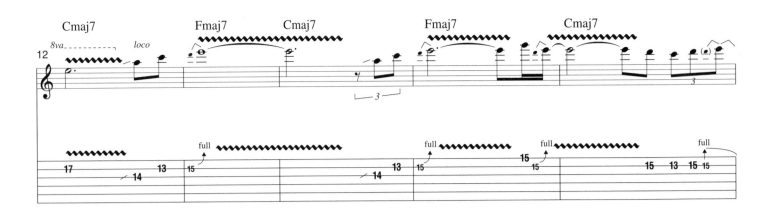

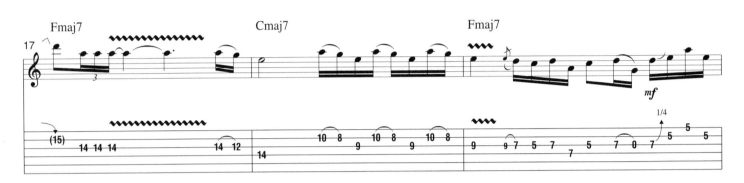

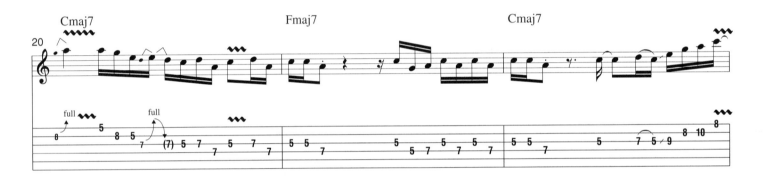

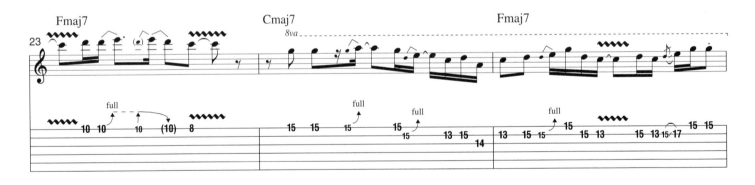

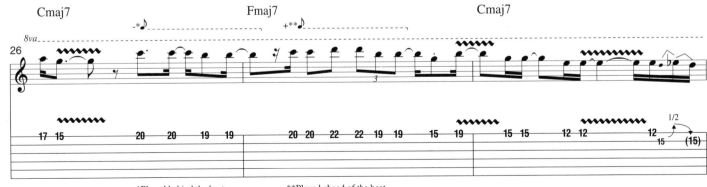

*Played behind the beat.   **Played ahead of the beat.

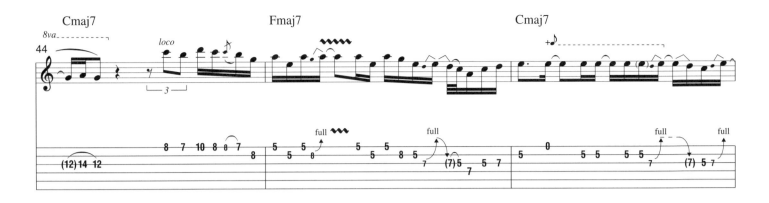

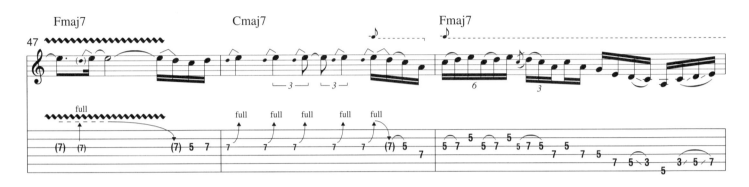

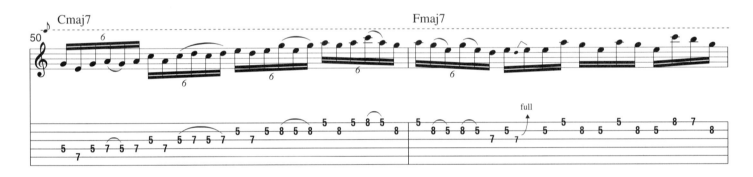

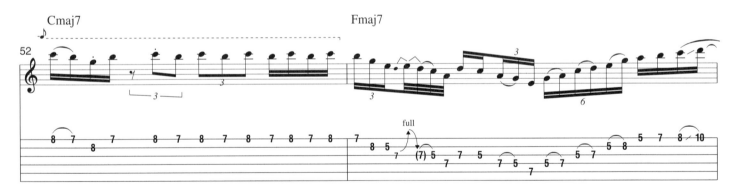

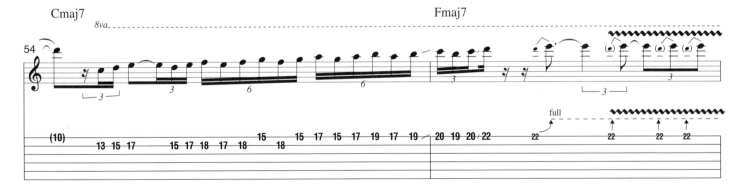

JESSICA
(As Performed by The Allman Brothers Band)
Words and Music by Dickey Betts

Figure 15 – Intro and Theme

The Allman Brothers Band was the major instigator of the southern-rock genre of the seventies, and one of the great rock acts of the era—and continues to be popular today. Originally a six-piece group, it was, among many things, a showcase for the twin-lead guitar work of Duane Allman and Dickey Betts. One of the finest pieces to exemplify the sound was Betts's composition "Jessica" from 1973's *Brothers and Sisters* album. A classic Allman Brothers instrumental exploiting the signature twin-lead approach, "Jessica" represents the natural evolution of their unique blues, rock, country, jazz, and gospel roots in one tight, guitar-oriented package. Betts played both parts of the twin-lead sections as it was recorded after Duane Allman's untimely death.

"Jessica" grows out of Betts's driving acoustic guitar riff (on Gtr. 1) in the intro [A]. The memorable theme [B] begins in measure 8. This is a soaring, arpeggio-based melody played in parallel diatonic harmony by Gtrs. 2 and 3. It is based on country-inflected A major sounds, leaning toward the A major pentatonic scale (A–B–C#–E–F#) with the addition of a D note used prominently in the line. The main melody is played by Gtr. 2 and is harmonized by Gtr. 3 with the appropriate chord/scale tone either a diatonic third or fourth above. The lines are decorated with slinky string bends, bluesy vibrato, and legato phrasing.

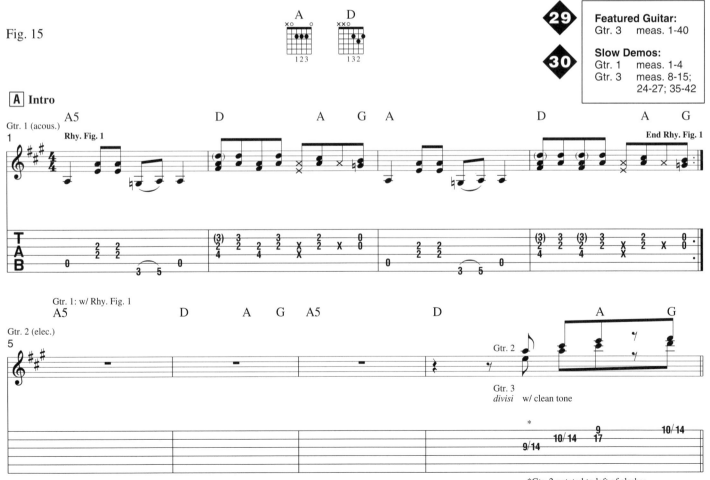

LENNY
(As Performed by Stevie Ray Vaughan)
By Stevie Ray Vaughan

Figure 16 – Intro, Head, and Guitar Solo

Stevie Ray Vaughan was, and still is, the incontestable blues champion of the modern age. Since his initial public appearance in the early eighties, no other player has made such a significant or lasting impact on the blues genre. His stature grew to mythical proportions in the relatively short span of his career and he now occupies an auspicious place in the pantheon of guitar gods—alongside his personal heroes B.B., Freddy and Albert King, Jimi Hendrix, Buddy Guy, and Wes Montgomery.

"Lenny" is a signature Stevie Ray Vaughan tune and reinstates the viability of the guitar instrumental in the 1980s—and its infusion into modern blues and rock genres. A moody ballad from Vaughan's classic 1983 debut album *Texas Flood*, the composition was named after his wife at the time, and presented the flamboyant Texas bluesman in a dramatically different setting. "Lenny" is set in a slow, floating tempo, contains a haunting chord-melody head, and is a simultaneous tribute to several of his influences: Jimi Hendrix, Curtis Mayfield, and Wes Montgomery. The intro [A] and head [B] are clearly jazz-inflected. The use of Emaj13 and A6 in the main chord figure in measures 4–17 takes the normal I to IV change into more extended harmonic territory. The jazz element is further heightened by the uncommon modulating progression of B6–D6–G6–B♭6–A6 in measures 20–27. By contrast, the fills in the intro and head are based on the R&B chord-melody approach of Mayfield and Hendrix. Throughout the intro and head Stevie shakes the chords with the vibrato bar (à la the Ventures) for a quasi-Hawaiian effect and uses a sensitive fingerstyle articulation.

Stevie's solos take place over a repeating E to A (I to IV) progression. His first solo [C] contains a well-balanced mixture of scales. He begins with lines based on the E major pentatonic scale (E–F#–G#–B–C#) in measures 35–38. The melody in measures 39–43 has a contrasting minor tonality emphasized by the G note in the phrases. Note the use of fingerplucking technique to play a classic pedal-tone blues lick in measures 39 and 40. Vaughan exploits both the minor and major 3rd (G and G#) in measures 44 and 45. Double stops are pursued in measures 47–50 and the B♭ from the E blues scale (E–G–A–B♭–B–D) figures prominently in the phrase. Stevie alludes to his idol Albert King in measures 52–53. He plays an interesting mixed-mode line in measures 55–59 to close the solo. Notice the inclusion of the minor and major 3rd (G and G#), the 6th (C#), 7th (D), and ♭5th (B♭) in the phrase. The intervallic melody in measures 57-58 is a highlight of the solo.

Stevie Ray Vaughan played "Lenny" on a unique yellow '64 Fender Stratocaster. Nicknamed Lenny (also after his wife), this Strat was hollowed out at one time for four humbuckers and was later restored by Charley Wirz. At this point in his career, Stevie plugged into Fender amps, either Vibroverbs, or Super Reverbs.

[Before playing along with Fig. 16, tune down 1/2 step with track 7]

Fig. 16

Tune Down 1/2 Step:

① = E♭ ④ = D♭

② = B♭ ⑤ = A♭

③ = G♭ ⑥ = E♭

31 **32**

Featured Guitar:
Gtr. 1 meas. 1-77

Slow Demos:
Gtr. 1 meas. 1-12; 16-28; 35-60

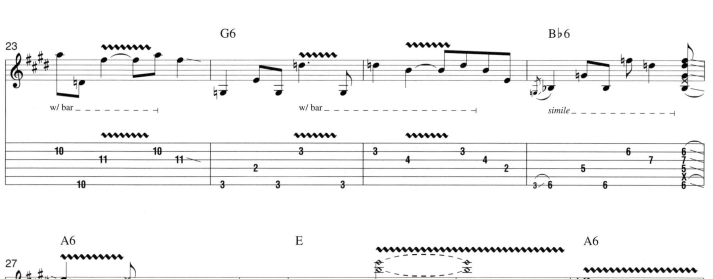

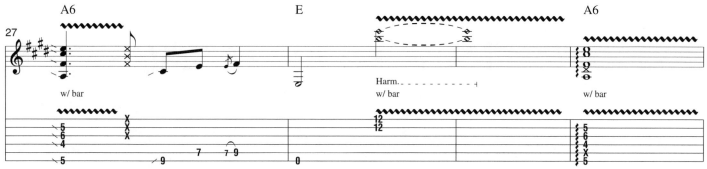

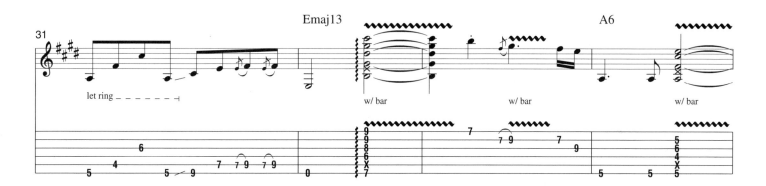

*Chords implied by bass & previous changes.

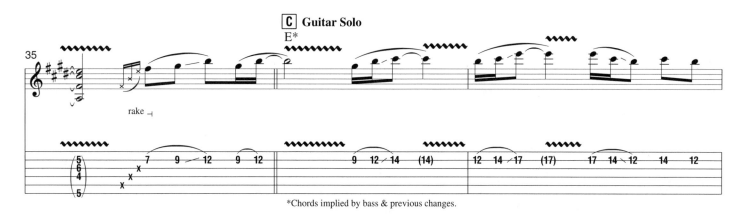

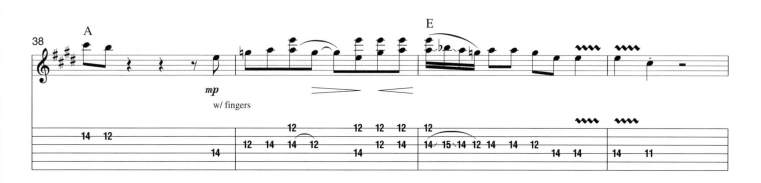

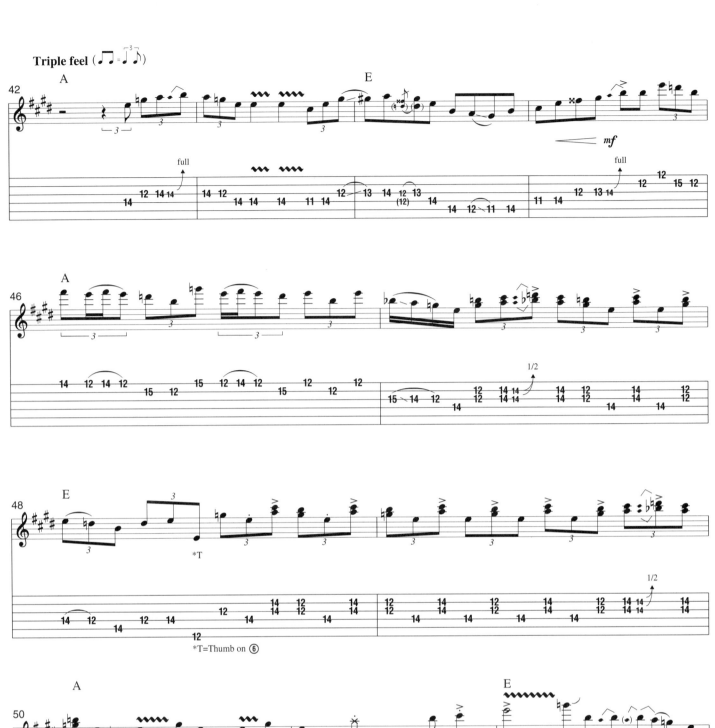

*T=Thumb on ⑥

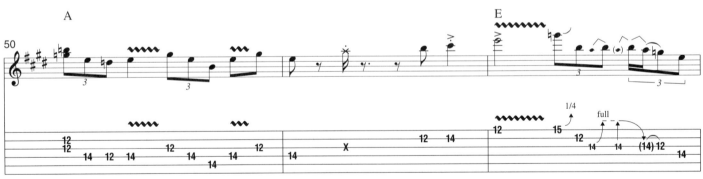

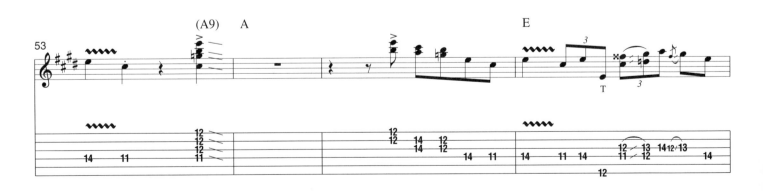

FROSTY
(As Performed by Albert Collins and B.B. King)
By Albert Collins

Figure 17—Head and Guitar Solos

Texas bluesman Albert Collins was appropriately known as "the Iceman" and "the master of the Telecaster," and had a well-earned reputation for stopping listeners cold in their tracks. With a chilling ice-pick attack, he gained wide recognition among blues fans and guitar players alike via his namesake instrumental, "Frosty," in 1962. There are numerous versions of "Frosty" in the Collins catalog. This one is significant for several reasons. Recorded in May 1993, it is from his last studio album, *Collins Mix*, and features a guest appearance by B.B. King—one of only two historic pairings of Collins and King on record. The session came about as a result of swapping favors. While in town, Albert sat in with B.B. on his *Blues Summit* album and, in return, asked King to perform on his record. What we get is a spirited and inspired romp through the Iceman's classic blues tune with remarkable guitar work by both players, both of whom were in top form for this date.

"Frosty" is an uptempo 12-bar blues in D. Collins takes the head [A] and first two solo choruses [B] and [C], followed by King for two [D] and [E]. Albert then returns with one more chorus [F] to close out the section with authority. The alternating 12-measure solos provide a fascinating study of Collins's and King's individual styles. Both swing unbelievably. Collins has a snappy, rhythmic-based style, plays aggressively—slightly ahead or on top of the beat—with a piercing tone, and consistently employs a slick variant of the standard minor pentatonic scale. Found throughout the head and solos, it involves replacing the 7th of the minor pentatonic (C) with the major 6th (B). "Albert's D minor pentatonic" is thus spelled D–F–G–A–B. This lends a jazzy, diminished sound to the arpeggio lines he favors over the typical pentatonic scale licks of most blues guitarists. The trill figures in [B] measure 5 and [C] measures 9–10, and the repeating bend passages in [B] measures 11–12 and [F] measures 1–4 are further definitive Albert Collins stylistic traits.

By contrast, King plays with a more relaxed—majestic—rhythmic approach and a fatter Lucille (ES-355) tone. Spurred on by "Frosty"'s cool environment, he also incorporates the 6th into his minor pentatonic phrases. Notice also the frequent inclusion of the 9th (E) in his lines in [D] measures 1–6, and [E] measures 1–3. A high point is the energetic, raked arpeggio riff in [E] measures 5–7.

Practically nothing is conventional about Albert Collins's style and technique. He tuned his Tele up to an open F minor chord (from low to high: F–C–F–A♭–C–F), always used a capo (generally at the 9th fret), and hung his guitar off his right shoulder. He picked exclusively with his fingers for a variety of attacks, nuance, and dynamics.

Albert's trademark guitar was a blonde, maple-neck '61 Telecaster with a humbucking neck pickup. He had been playing them since 1952, when "Gatemouth" Brown first turned him on to them, and was one of the first blues legends to play a modified Tele. Collins plugged into mid-1970s Fender Quad Reverb combo amps—each essentially a "100-watt stack in a box."

Fig. 17

Featured Guitars:
Gtr. 1 [A] - [C] meas. 1-12
Gtr. 2 [D] - [E] meas. 1-12
Gtr. 1 [F] meas. 1-12

Slow Demos:
Gtr. 1 [A] - [C] meas. 1-12
Gtr. 2 [D] - [E] meas. 1-12
Gtr. 1 [F] meas. 1-12

*Open F minor tuning adapted for standard tuning.